THE POWER OF FIVE

BY LA'SHEA CRETAIN

Copyright © 2020 La'Shea Cretain

All rights reserved.

ISBN: 978-1-7344392-1-2

DEDICATION

This book is dedicated to my strong, beautiful children Donte and Shayla. You inspire me every single day. I would also like to dedicate it to my whole, big family. Thank you for always standing by me. Finally, I would like to dedicate it to all of the leaders, like Shannon Watts, Ms. B, and others who take time out of their own busy lives to step up for others. Thank you for making our world a better place.

CONTENTS

1: UNLIKELY ACTIVIST 1

2: SHOT 3

3: A STATISTIC 6

4: SURVIVAL 8

5: FAITH 12

6: FIGHT 16

7: FORGET 23

8: FORGIVE 27

9: FAMILY 37

10: FUTURE 43

11: FAREWELL FOR NOW 67

ABOUT THE AUTHOR 69

REFERENCE 104

1

UNLIKELY ACTIVIST

Speaking at Atlanta GSU in 2018

My name is La'Shea Cretain. Like millions of Americans, I am a gun violence survivor.

A few years back, my daughter Shayla and I were kicking back, watching *Keeping up with the Kardashians* - like you do on a lazy Sunday afternoon. It happened to be an episode where Kim was talking about her passion for gun sense laws, and her work with a group called Everytown for Gun Safety. Shayla turned to me and said, "You have to look into the group that Kim is talking about."

It had never really occurred to me that my story could help anyone else. I never considered myself an activist or an advocate, but when I looked up Everytown, and their other group, Moms Demand Action for Gun Sense in America, I realized that that this was something I had to do.

Since joining Moms and Everytown, I've told my story at many events all across the country. My story has been printed in *Time Magazine, the New York Times, and Vogue,* along with many other publications. I am living with five bullets inside my body, but as I said in my quote recently for artist Jenny Holzer's installation in New York City, I consider myself lucky compared with people who have lost their loved ones to gun violence.

It's not always easy for me to tell my story. It's hard for me to relive it time and time again. It takes a physical toll on my body to stand for long periods of time. But my hope is that, by sharing my story here, I can help someone else overcome their own trials. Because despite all the things that divide us, there is one thing that unites us – we will all face our own challenges at some point. This is the story of how I discovered the Power of Five inside of myself to help me heal and fight my way back from being shot by my ex-boyfriend. I hope that those powers can help give you strength, too.

2

SHOT

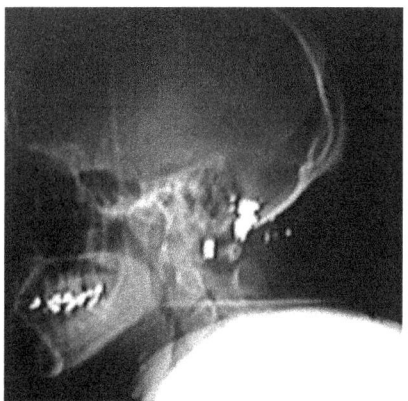

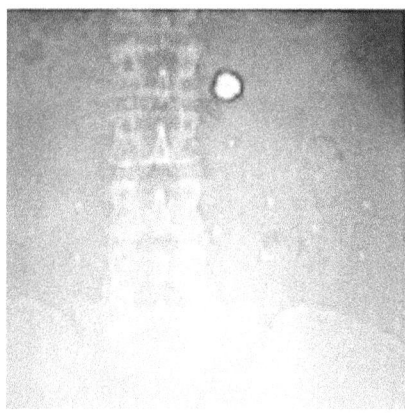

2013 X-Ray taken in San Diego, CA.

I remember waking up the morning of October 3, 1996 thinking it was going to be a good day. The hot, humid Louisiana summer was finally breaking. Sunlight and a slight breeze were drifting in through the window at my Great Aunt's house. My baby girl was sleeping peacefully beside me. Her big brother was resting across the room beside my Great Aunt. My dad had bought a car for me for graduation a few months earlier. He had been doing a little work on it, but he was bringing it to my Aunt's house later that day. I couldn't wait to have that freedom. I was planning where to begin my new life with my babies. Little did I know that in a few hours, I would be shot.

My Aunt and I had a great day together. I've always loved kids and even though I was ashamed at times to have two babies from two different fathers by the time I was eighteen, I loved my kids with all my heart. I was determined to be a good mother. But that afternoon, as I walked to my Great Aunt's front door, my body was full of dread. My ex Ricky Jr. was there, waiting for me. I was so tired of fighting. I'd broken up with him a year earlier, due to his mood swings and our volatile relationship. But he wouldn't take no for an answer.

Ricky Jr. had already stopped by earlier that day and slapped me. I did not want to see him again, but his mother Mrs. C had come to the house, begging me to talk to her son. He was threatening to take his own life. My Great Aunt and I had just finished feeding my four-month old daughter Shayla and my almost two-year old son Donte. I went to the door and faced Ricky Jr. through the glass screen. I told him once again that it was over and that I didn't want to open the door or go anywhere with him. The last words I said to him were, "Ricky, I love you. You can have the kids whenever you want, but I can't be with you."

I turned to walk away and I heard a pop, pop, pop behind me, and the sound of shattering glass. The next thing I knew, I was down on the floor. It felt like something warm and sticky was trickling down over the side of my face. That's all I could feel, the rest of my body had gone completely numb. And all I could think about was worrying if my babies were okay.

I didn't know it yet, but Ricky Jr. had just shot five bullets into my body. Five bullets that could have killed my babies or someone else I loved. Five bullets that would change my life forever.

Three of the bullets lodged near my spine at the base of my skull. Two pierced me on either side of my back, passing through to my abdomen and damaging my colon. Due to their placement, the doctors had to leave the bullets inside of me. In time, I would come to name those bullets for everything it took for me to recover – FAITH, FIGHT, FORGET, FORGIVE and FAMILY. But first, I had to find the strength to stay alive.

3

A STATISTIC

High School Graduation Photo, 1996

The day Ricky Jr. shot me, and then turned the gun around and killed himself, we both became a statistic. According to the Brady Project, 310 people are shot in this country every single day. Like me, 95 people are injured in an attack with a gun, and like Ricky Jr., 61 people die every day from suicide using a gun.

I didn't know until quite recently that even before I was shot, my family had already been affected by gun violence. Like many rural families, my mom and dad had me when they were very young. Their relationship didn't last long. To make ends meet, my mom was working as a checker at a convenience store in our small town. A local man she recognized came in and robbed the store at gunpoint. After my mom testified against the robber, she was forced to leave town for her own safety. She had to choose between bringing me to a strange town, without any family support - or leaving me to live with my grandparents. I grew up with my grandparents, never realizing that my mom was forced to leave me behind for my own safety.

Ricky Jr. and I were a statistic in other ways. I'm not proud of it, but Ricky Jr. and I had a long history of fighting. Like so many other women, I was a victim of domestic violence before I was shot. Many abusive relationships end in gun violence. According to an article by *Mother Jones*, a history of domestic violence is also one of the most common factors in the personal histories of mass shooters. Of the 22 mass shooters *Mother Jones* researched, 86% had a history of domestic violence.

Sadly, we are just one of the many families who have been affected by gun violence in this country.

4

❖

SURVIVAL

January, 1997. Thrilled to be with my babies three months after the shooting.

I have no idea how long I was on the floor waiting for help. According to the police report, my Great Aunt called 911 at 2:48pm. She grabbed hold of my son Donte and held him tight, then went to my daughter Shayla and called the police. I didn't know for sure at the time, but my babies were safe. All five of the bullets Ricky Jr. shot went into me.

As they carried me out the door on a stretcher, I understood how people feel when they talk about seeing a light at the moment of death. The afternoon sun seemed so impossibly bright to me. I could hear voices all around me, but somehow they seemed very far away. "Can you move your toes?" I heard them say. "Stay with us, La'Shea."

I tried to tell them that I was fine, that I was right there, but I couldn't find my voice. I tried to tell them that I was moving my toes, but I couldn't feel my body. I fought to stay awake, but the light was too powerful and bright, Finally, I had to close my eyes. Away from the light, into the darkness.

For some time after Ricky Jr. shot me, I was in a coma. I felt like I was in a strange shadowy room, bustling with people all around me – like a flea market located somewhere in the grey area between life and death. I could hear people coming and going around me, but I could not speak to them. I didn't realize it at the time, but they had brought me back to the same hospital where I had given birth to my son Donte just a few years earlier.

As I drifted in that shadowy room, there were many times I wanted to surrender to the darkness. It seemed so peaceful there. But every time I was tempted to give up, I thought about my babies, Shayla and Donte. I wanted to get back to them and hold them so much, so I kept fighting my way towards the light. I felt so tired. Tired from all of the fighting with Ricky Jr. Tired from finishing school and from trying to raise my two babies alone. Tired from working two jobs to survive, and tired from trying to fight off the heavy weight that seemed to be filling my lungs.

As I lay still in a thick fog in my hospital bed, I heard many voices talking around me. I could hear the doctors and nurses passing in and out of my room I could hear my family. Hundreds of my friends came to visit. Even though I couldn't speak to them, their voices and presence meant the world to me.

Through my haze, I heard my mother's voice arguing with my father and the doctors. All those years I had spent as a little girl, wishing my parents would get back together, now here they were by my side. Aside from my high school graduation a few months earlier, this was the first time my parents had been together with me in years. My mom had traveled with her cousin in an 18-wheeler all the way from Detroit, Michigan to be with me.

When she was younger, my mom had studied to be a nurse. She wasn't able to finish her schooling, but she had learned enough to know how much trouble I was in. I could hear her arguing with my father and the doctor. "She NEEDS to breathe," my mom said.

Sometimes you need love and support from your family, but other times, you need them to fight for you. I could hear the alarm in my mother's voice and I wanted to tell her I was okay, but it felt like the weight of the world was pressing down on my chest. I heard the doctor say 'pneumonia' and I understood that I was having a hard time breathing on my own. I could hear the heartbreak in my father's voice. I could only imagine how much it pained him to see me like that. He argued that they needed to give me time and allow me to get stronger, but my mother knew I was in dire straits. She told my dad that if I didn't start fighting to breathe for myself right then and there, the pneumonia was going to fill my lungs and I'd never draw another breath.

The last thing I remember before going under again was my mother's voice bossing everyone around and begging me, "Breathe, La'Shea, please. You have to breathe."

So, I did.

5

FAITH

High School Graduation, 1996

I am so grateful for both sides of my family. My mother's family raised me, but my dad and his family lived close by. My dad's mother was in nursing, and his father was a farmer. I had a lot of fun when my dad and uncles would take me out riding on my on grandpa's tractor through the cornfields. My aunts on my dad's side of the family used to pick me up for many special occasions. Growing up, I truly felt blessed to be surrounded by so much love on both sides.

My grandparents had already raised several children of their own when they took me in. In fact, they were still raising their eighth child alongside me. Although I was the oldest grandchild, I was the youngest child in the house for a long while - a spitfire with reddish-brown hair and an easy smile. I was physically precocious and always into everything. Truth be told, my family doted on me a lot, but I still had to fight to make myself heard in our big, boisterous family.

We were a drinking, smoking, fighting family, but there was also a lot of love. My family did everything big. By the time I came along, my grandparents had given up on church. They weren't anti-religion, but it was simply not a big part of our daily lives. My grandpa worked for the Sheriff's Department and my grandma worked as a cook. They were busy and tired a lot of the time, so I often ran wild, playing by myself in our backyard, or in the woods near our home. Even though I didn't go to church when I was little, I had a big imagination. Some part of me always longed for something bigger than the world I knew, and I always sensed a greater presence in those woods with me.

I was close to many of my Great Aunts, but one of them became a very important figure in my life. She was a true believer, and she sometimes took me with her and my cousins to their Catholic church. Truth be told, at that point I didn't love the long sermons, or sitting in the sticky Louisiana heat in my scratchy lace dresses, but those incredible stained glass windows and all of that pomp and ceremony definitely made an impression on me.

My Godmother gave me my first bible when I was a pre-teen. Eventually, I went to church with my Great Aunt often enough to attend catechism and participate in my First Communion. Looking back now, I realize that I found comfort in the words and the rituals, but as a child, I never quite connected with religion on a deeper level. I loved the social aspect of church, but I felt like the sermons went over my head instead of into my soul.

As I was lying in the hospital in my coma, I heard several voices around me, and felt something warm at my feet. My mom had brought my kids in to see me. I was on a feeding and breathing tube, and I had IV's from my head to my toes, so my mom had to tuck my daughter Shayla down near my feet. I heard my mom saying that Ricky Jr. had shot and killed himself. She had taken the kids to his funeral. I learned he was dead while I was trapped there, all on my own, fighting against the darkness. I had to process that all on my own. My breathing was slowly getting stronger, but I still couldn't move, or raise my voice.

Then, one day I heard my Great Aunt and my cousin's voices close by. "He restoreth my soul," I heard them say together. "He leadeth me in the paths of righteousness for his name's sake." Hearing their loving, familiar voices saying these words, something deep inside of me opened. It was as if all that weight that had been crushing down on my lungs lifted, and I could breathe in the light surrounding me and banish some of the darkness. I fought to wake up. "Yea, though I walk in the valley of the shadow of death, I will fear no evil, for thou art with me."

"God," I heard my own inner-voice speak. "Please, God. Let me walk and talk again," I begged. "Let me hold my babies and I promise, I will do your will." I felt the heaviness lift from my chest, like a light pouring into me, chasing out that dark grey fog I'd been hovering in during my coma.

Look, I want you to know right now, you don't have to believe in God to read this book. Faith has become an important part of my life, but I believe that faith comes to people in many forms. I have worshipped beside my Jewish and Muslim friends. I have had deep, soulful conversations with my atheist friends about humanity and the wonders of the universe. I have felt my soul vibrate to the beauty of nature, as it did when I was a little girl playing out in the woods. I am a Christian, but my faith is strong enough to acknowledge and respect other belief systems.

All I know is that finding my faith was the first step I needed to take in my healing. Faith is what led me out of the darkness when I was trying to fight my way out of my coma. I knew I wanted to get back to my children so badly, but it wasn't until I heard my loved ones there by my side, saying the words of the Shepherd's Prayer, that I discovered the light of hope inside myself.

6

FIGHT

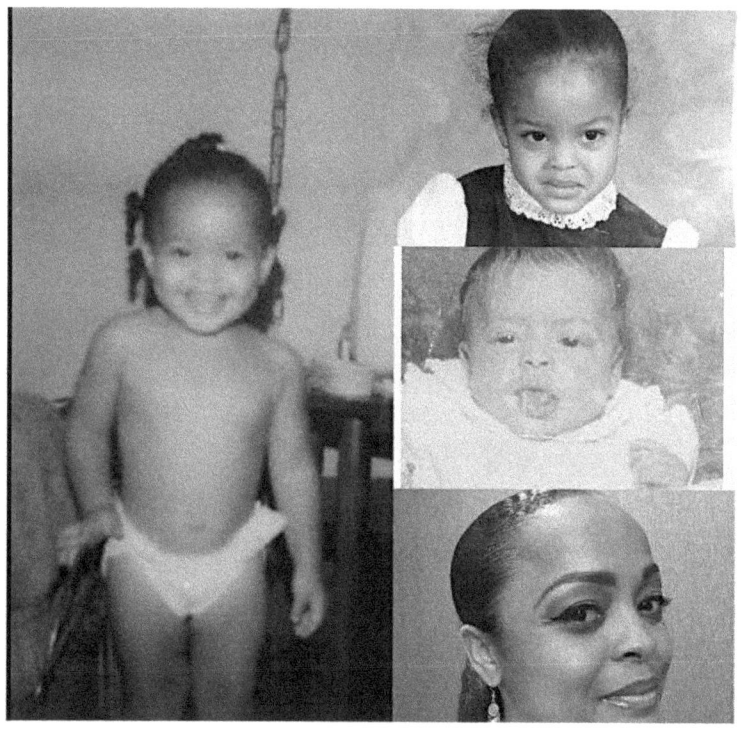

Collage of pictures from my childhood in Opelousas, Louisiana to now.

I was born a fighter.

I was a very active kid, I participated in lots of different sports, but when I was 8 years old, I began to feel heart palpitations. I sometimes had trouble catching my breath. After several scary incidents, I was diagnosed with a heart condition called Wolff-Parkinson-White Syndrome. I was just a little kid, but I had to have heart surgery to re-calibrate my heart. I remember being scared to go to the hospital, but more than anything, I wanted to regain my strength. I loved to move my body and I didn't want anything to slow me down – not even my own heart. My grandparents drove two hours away from our home to New Orleans for the surgery. They stayed at the hospital with me until I was ready to go home. I slowed down for a little while but soon I was back to my old, irrepressible self.

My grandparents grew up in the 1930's. They still remembered the hardscrabble life of their youth and they raised us to be thrifty and respectful. We chopped our own wood and caught fish from the streams near our home for my grandma to filet in the back yard, where I ran around, wild and free. In many ways, our small Louisiana town still felt like it was from a simpler time and place. Even though it was often idyllic there, in all that humid heat, the line between right and wrong could sometimes get blurred.

My grandfather worked for our local Sheriff's Department and he taught me early on how to defend myself. "Don't go looking for trouble," he would say. "But if someone else starts it, you be ready to finish it." As I said, my family did everything big – we loved passionately and fought hard. Despite my bubbly personality, I did not shy away from fights if someone started one with me. I was suspended twice at school for fighting back against a boy who kept picking on me. My family's fighting spirit serves me well in some ways, but it was also something I would eventually have to overcome.

NW High School Point Guard, 10th grade, 1994.

I was always a scrappy kid, but once my heart healed, I was unstoppable. My grandparents got me to focus all that excess energy on athletics. I excelled at dance, track and my favorite sport – basketball. I always felt in tune with my body. I could quickly pick up a dance routine, fly over hurtles and, despite my small frame, I could dribble and glide down a basketball court with the best of them.

That's how I met Ricky Jr. at school. Ricky Jr. was a beautiful 6' 4" basketball player. I fell for his deep eyes and shy smile, but I quickly learned that Ricky Jr. had a darker side. He was moody and possessive and his temper could escalate into violence. I'm not proud to say that I was a part of that cycle. If Ricky Jr. hit me, I hit back. We yelled at each other, threw things, pushed each other, the whole nine yards.

Finally, when I was a few months pregnant with our daughter Shayla, I saw Ricky Jr. pull a gun on my friend. Before that, I knew Ricky Jr. had mood swings and I knew he could be violent, but I didn't realize how far he might take it. Luckily, that altercation did not end in bloodshed, but it changed something in me. I was a fighter, but this wasn't who I wanted to be. I wanted to break this cycle of violence I was living in. I wanted to leave Ricky Jr. and move away from my home to start a new life with my babies. I broke up with Ricky Jr., but he refused to let go.

Although I happened to be staying at my Great Aunt's house the day Ricky Jr. shot me, I was still living with my grandparents at that time. I was only 18 and already had two children, but I was a hard worker. I had recently graduated from high school and was working two jobs to support my family. My Dad was a mechanic who worked close to my Great Aunt's house. He didn't raise me, but he was always a big part of my life. I was at my Great Aunt's house waiting for my dad to bring the car he'd fixed up to help me start my new life.

My Great Aunt is a strong woman. We have an easy rapport and we laughed and enjoyed each other's company that day as we prepared food and looked after the children together. Just as we were setting the table for lunch, there was a powerful knock at the door. It was too early to be my father. I went to answer the door and found Ricky Jr. standing on the porch.

Ricky Jr. followed me into my Aunt's home and begged me to leave with him and go talk. I told him that I didn't want to go anywhere with him - he needed to accept that we were over. Ricky Jr. slapped me. My Aunt came into the room to find me pummeling him and telling him to leave. She held my two children close and firmly told Ricky Jr. that he had to go.

Ricky Jr. left, and I ran to the bathroom in tears. I didn't like the person Ricky Jr. was when he became violent – but, more importantly – I didn't like the person I became around him. I was so sad and scared and ashamed, I felt sick to my stomach. My Great Aunt asked me through the door if I was okay and I told her, "I'm just so tired of fighting, I don't want to do it, anymore." I didn't want my babies to grow up around that kind of aggression.

My Great Aunt soothed me and we finished serving lunch to the little ones. A little while later, the phone rang. It was Mrs. C, Ricky Jr.'s mother. I could hear the alarm in her voice. She begged me to please come over and talk to Ricky Jr. He had a gun and she was worried he might hurt himself. I told her I was sorry, but that I wasn't going anywhere near Ricky Jr. I hung up the phone, but Ricky Jr. only lived twenty minutes away. A short while later, there was a softer knock at the door. This time, it was Ricky Jr.'s mom on my Great Aunt's doorstep.

As she pleaded with me to come and talk to Ricky Jr., I felt for her. I could sense her desperation and love for her son, but I was a mother, myself. The wellbeing of my own children had to take priority, and I could not take on the responsibility for someone else's life. We heard a knock at the door – it was Ricky Jr. He'd parked at a little ways up the street, so we hadn't heard him arrive. Mrs. C pleaded with me to talk to him, but I reiterated that I did not want to see him.

Ricky Jr.'s mother went out to try to calm him down. He walked down the road a little and she came back in to talk to me, but pretty soon he returned. He wasn't going to take no for an answer. She reasoned with him, but he refused to back down. She came back inside and begged me to please talk to him. Reluctantly, I went to meet him at my Great Aunt's front door. I kept the glass screen closed between us. I did not want him to hurt me again. But a glass screen door wasn't enough to protect me from what was coming. As soon as I turned to walk away, Ricky shot me five times.

My pictures from high school show a happy, carefree girl with a full life ahead of her. But now, at only 18-years old, I found myself lying on the floor, with five bullets in my body. I didn't realize it then, but my fighting spirit was already working to save my life. All of the sports I'd excelled in had conditioned my body to survive the worst. All of my strength and determination was now focused on protecting my children, and keeping me alive so I could fight my way back to them.

Mrs. C came crawling towards me in a panic. "La'Shea?! Are you okay?"

"Get Donte," I heard my own voice. I knew Shayla was partially protected, but Donte had been running free just moments before, as toddlers do. I worried he would run towards me and into the line of fire.

But Mrs. C didn't seem to hear me. She looked over my head in anguish and said, "Oh my God, he's shot himself." She didn't hear my plea for my son because her own son had just taken his life outside. She ran past me out the door to Ricky Jr.

7

FORGET

Family photo, Christmas, 2001. San Diego, California

The officers who came to the house the day I was shot listed me as a 'victim' on their police report. They did not expect me to survive the drive to the hospital. While I was in surgery, the hospital told my family that I probably would not live.

But God answered my prayers. After my Great Aunt and my cousin's visit, just a week after being shot, I woke up from my coma. Waking up was a struggle, but my real battle was just beginning. I still had all five bullets in my body.

I had to undergo several surgeries, including surgery to save my colon. Miraculously, I survived. But because of the placement of the bullets, the doctors could not remove them during my surgeries. I had staples in my stomach from the surgery and had to wear a diaper during my recovery.

I will never forget when my dad's oldest sister came in my hospital room tended to my hair while I was recovering. I couldn't wash my hair, but she gently combed the blood and tangles out of my hair. She put my hair in braids, the way she used to do when I was little girl.

They warned my family that there was a good chance I would never walk again. I'd already surprised them by talking so quickly. Despite my crippling pain, I was determined to fulfill my next goal - I wanted to walk back into my home and hold my babies. I fought to regain my strength. Within a few days, I was going to the bathroom with help from the nurses. Although I still had to use a wheelchair most of the time, I was up and walking the hospital hallways every chance I got.

I had to forget a lot of things during that time. I had to forget my physical pain. I had to forget how scared and out of control I felt during my relationship with Ricky Jr. I had to forget how close he came to killing me, and my babies. I had to forget that the police and doctors did not expect me to survive.

I don't know if it's possible to ever completely forget the traumas we endure. But I refused to let them consume me in those early days. I wanted to stay positive and stay focused on healing and getting stronger. As the years have passed, I have found that the old adage 'time heals all wounds' resonates for a reason. The scars on my body from being shot five times will be with me forever, but I won't let them define me.

A week and a half after Ricky Jr. shot me; I was released from the hospital. Surrounded by my loved ones, I walked into my grandparents' house, just like I had prayed – no more wheelchair. I couldn't hold my babies yet, but I got to sleep with them. My wiggly toddler Donte kicked me so hard in his sleep, he loosened the staples in my stomach. I had to go back to the doctor almost immediately, but I refused to let them separate us. On November 30 - my son's birthday - I was able to hold my babies for the first time since the shooting. I had a smile on my face as big and bright as the sun. I was truly beginning to heal. My staples were taken out for good that December.

In recent years, I wanted to uncover the mystery of my own attack. I fought hard for the right to review the police report from the day I was shot. It took me more than twenty years to receive a copy of it. The police could not find my file. They would not give me very much information about Ricky Jr. since I was not his wife. A friend suggested that I contact the District Attorney.

It turned out, the responding officers had noted the wrong date on the report. They had entered October 2nd, but according to the hospital records, I was brought in on October 3rd. Finally, with the District Attorney's help, I was given a copy of the police report from the day I was shot. My injuries were so severe; the officers on the scene had listed me as a "victim". I can only imagine that they thought I would die on the way to the hospital. But to me, it was incredibly painful to read that report. I'm not dead; I am still very much alive. And I choose to live in joy and love.

In order to do that, I had to forget the look in Ricky Jr.'s eyes right before I turned around and he shot me five times. I had to forget the pain that still sears through my body at times, and the aftershocks of dread that I still feel knowing how easily our lives can be shattered in an instant. I had to forget how hard it was for me to get to this point in my life. Instead, I decided to focus on all of my blessings.

I found out from the police report that Ricky Jr. left a note in his mother's car before he killed himself. She recently told me that she still has that note today. One gunshot can impact so many lives.

8

FORGIVE

Family photo, Christmas, 2001. San Diego, California

I'm a positive person. I was a happy little girl and an enthusiastic member of my school's band. After I got out of the hospital, I was so happy to be home with my family, but I knew I had to find my way forward. I had focused so much on forgetting my pain. Once I was home, I realized I still had a lot to forgive. I had to forgive the police for not helping me when I went to them shortly before Ricky Jr. shot me to tell them that I was scared of him. I had to forgive them for telling me there was nothing they could do. I had to forgive my own family's history of domestic abuse and silence. I had to forgive all of the people who told me I just had to stand by my man, no matter how many times he hit me. I had to forgive Ricky Jr. for not being able to conquer his demons. I had to forgive him for hurting me, and for putting my children and loved ones at risk. I had to forgive him for taking his own life, and leaving our daughter without a father. Most of all, I had to forgive myself. I had to forgive myself for fighting and getting physical with Ricky Jr. I had to forgive myself for not cutting things off with him sooner. I had to forgive myself for not trusting my instincts and getting far away from him.

My faith was still a little rough in those early days. But I prayed all the time for the strength to forgive and to move forward with my life. In order to do that, I knew I needed to take my children somewhere new, somewhere without so many painful memories.

In February of 1999, I packed my kids in the car my daddy fixed up for me for my graduation and we moved to Florida to live with my Godmother.

My Godmother worked for the Navy. The orderliness and relative quiet of her home was just what my kids and I needed while we recovered. She really helped me get back on my feet. I got a job at McDonald's and worked hard, saving money while I was living with her. Eventually, I saved up enough to buy a new car for my family – a 1999 Toyota Corolla. I was as excited about that car as most people would be about a Mercedes. I earned it, myself. When my Godmother shipped out later that year, I decided to move the kids once again. I wanted to live somewhere close to family, so we relocated to San Diego, CA to live with my Aunt and Uncle.

I had a history in San Diego. When I was little, my mom had re-married a military man and relocated to San Diego. They stayed with my Aunt and Uncle, and I went to live them for a little while. My stepdad was born and raised in Detroit, and loved basketball. Eventually, my mom sent me back to my family in Louisiana and she moved to Detroit with her husband.

In 7th grade, I went to Detroit to live with my mom and stepdad, but I was crushed to discover that they had divorced. I returned to San Diego briefly, expecting to attend high school there. My uncle had been diagnosed with brain cancer, and my grandma had flown out to help care for him. Unfortunately, he fell in the bathtub and was rushed to the hospital, but he never recovered.

I loved my uncle dearly. He was the baby of the family, and he always treated me like his little sis. We grew up like siblings, playing together all the time. I visited him daily in the hospital while he was on life support. All I wanted to do was go outside and play sports with him, but that would never happen again. My family flew his body back home for his funeral, and I returned with him.

After my uncle's death, things changed a lot in my grandparents' household. They fought all the time over his death. It was really hard for them to lose their baby, but I was still there. I missed him a lot and I felt really alone. My uncle used to talk to me about school, but neither of my grandparents finished college, so I was pretty much on my own. I think that's a big part of why I was so excited to have a boyfriend, and why I rushed into things with two different boys during high school. I didn't want to feel so alone.

Even though I was not able to finish school in San Diego, as I'd hoped, I always had fond memories of my time living there with my aunt and my uncle. It felt like the perfect place to go with my babies for a fresh start.

Straight talk right here – being a single mother is hard. I'd had my staples taken out in December and I was back to work by January. Even though I was working very hard to support us in those early years, I made sure that my kids were in a good daycare when they were little. That was my first priority. I wanted Donte and Shayla to have as many opportunities in life as possible.

When we moved to San Diego, I arranged my work schedule so that Donte and Shayla could participate in sports and other activities that interested them. As they grew older, Donte excelled in basketball, football and debate. Shayla also discovered a passion for debate, as well as becoming a talented dancer and performer. I was dog-tired a lot of the time. It felt like we were constantly schlepping from one activity to another, but I wouldn't change a single second of that time. When I was in a coma, all I could think about was getting back to my babies. That old saying about raising kids is true – the days are long, but the years are short. Cherish every minute of it, because they get big before you know it.

After two failed romantic relationships, part of my forgetting and forgiving process also involved learning new tools so that I could break that cycle for good. Eventually, I was able to get my own home with my children. I never lived with a man, and I strictly limited the guys I dated in front of my children. After the shooting, I made sure that I would never argue with a man in front of my children again. I very rarely drink, and only take a little Motrin now and then for my pain.

I was still working to forget some of my anger, so I decided to turn that anger into action. Aside from coaching some of my kids' teams, I also worked hard to stay physical, myself. I knew I couldn't run or do all the things I did when I was younger, but I figured that I ran enough when I was little for an entire lifetime! So I began to walk and do other gentle forms of exercise. I also do saunas and massage to help alleviate my pain and stress. Exercise has always been a big part of my life. I think it's a form of self-care. I'm not going to get too preachy about it, but if you're feeling stuck, try to get yourself moving. It can be something gentle, like walking, or yoga. Moving your body shifts your mood.

I was working hard while I was raising my babies, but I was also looking for other ways to channel my passion and energy. Shayla's love of performing eventually led to her getting involved with a Baptist church in our neighborhood. I didn't know what to expect the first time that we went. Despite my epiphany during my coma, I still hadn't fully connected with religion in a meaningful way. Although I love my Great Aunt and am so grateful for the foundation she gave me in the Catholic Church, I realized that I never quite felt at home there. Suddenly, this new church, full of song and families and life, felt familiar and welcoming.

One parishioner in particular would become a very important figure to me. Ms. B welcomed all of us with open arms. She taught me that there is no room for judgment in spirituality. In this new church, I never felt ashamed of having two kids by two different fathers, or of being a single mother. Little by little, the church became a bigger part of our lives. First I volunteered my accounting skills to the church. I've always been good with figures and it felt good to be able to give something back.

Ms. B could see that I had a natural bond with little kids. She encouraged me to volunteer with the children. Working with the kids in the Baptist church brought me so much joy and allowed me to do meaningful work, as well as giving me the opportunity to spend time with my own children while they were growing. My kids and I had finally found our spiritual home.

Never underestimate how big a difference one kind person can make in someone's life. I'm very fortunate to have so many loving people who have supported me over the years, but Ms. B truly became like a mentor and a grandmother to me. Now I know religion isn't for everyone. If it's not for you, that's just fine. But I think the lessons Ms. B taught me are profound no matter what you believe. Try not to judge other people. We never know what someone else is going through. Also, look for the good in people and try to support each other. This world is tough enough. Let's be kind to each other.

When I first moved to San Diego, I felt a little lost. By the time I was 18, I had two children. I wasn't ready for kids, and I definitely wasn't ready to be shot. How do you move on from that? I knew that I wanted to make a good life for my kids, but I didn't know what that looked like, or if I had the strength. I was still really struggling with a lot of residual fear and sadness.

I paid for all of my schooling and medical treatments, myself. I managed to earn a BSA, and am nearly finished with my MBA, all while raising two kids and working full time. I had to make sure I had insurance, and could take care of my kids on my own. Luckily, my kids also took care of me. They could see my struggles, so they always did extra chores to help me around the house. I drove them to all their sports and extra-curricular activities, but when they were old enough, they drove me to all of my medical appointments.

That's why I am so grateful that my children and I found a church that felt like home. We didn't have counseling, but our church community gave us a lot of support and healing. Ms. B made me feel like she heard me and knew my heart. She didn't question my path before coming to her church; she just welcomed me in and made me feel accepted. Religion is so important for me, but I don't think I truly understood it until I met Ms. B. She taught me how to forgive myself and how to accept others. We can't pass judgment on someone else. No one would choose to have two kids by 18, with no support, but if I hadn't had kids, I honestly don't know if I would be here today. I don't know if I would have fought as hard as I did to stay alive.

I've always loved children. I started out as the youngest in our house, but as my Aunts and Uncles got older and got married, we started to have more and more babies in our big family. By the time I was a teenager, I was on babysitting duty a lot of the time and I loved it. Kids are full of joy and mischief and discovery and being around them made me feel like I had a purpose. Within a year after Ms. B asked me to help out in Sunday School, I was promoted to Vacation Bible School Director. I experienced so much happiness and fulfillment working with those kids and watching my own children grow. It was a powerful reminder to play to your strengths. Think about what you love - how can you turn that into a volunteer or employment opportunity? I truly believe that the key to a happy life is to connect with your community.

One day, Ms. B invited me to a performance at her granddaughter's school. I was so impressed by the dedication of the staff and kindness of the students at Horizon Christian Academy, the next year I enrolled my 3rd and 4th grade children there. That became like a second home to us, as well.

Little by little, I could feel a tightness inside of me begin to let go. Part of the forgiving and forgetting process is the knowledge and wisdom that comes with age. Whenever we went back home to visit, I always took Shayla to bring flowers to her daddy's grave. Whatever happened between the two of us, Ricky Jr. was her father, and I wanted to make sure she felt the power of that connection. I had grown up mostly without my parents – I knew how hard that can be. It was difficult for me to stand there close to Ricky Jr.'s grave on those visits and not surrender to my anger and fear. But my love for my children was bigger than any memory, no matter how painful. I made sure that Shayla knew that even though her father was very troubled, he loved her.

I refused to let my past struggles dominate our lives, but I was honest with my kids about everything. I'm proud to say that Shayla chose to study criminal justice and sociology in college. She asked me to assist her with her senior project in college, interviewing me about the shooting and my experience. We received an A on her domestic violence project. Together, I am working with my kids to break the cycle of violence that too many families repeat generation after generation. If you are struggling with domestic violence, or any other big life challenge, I want you to know that you have the power within you to change your story.

Three months prior to her graduation from college, Shayla asked me to go and visit Ricky Jr.'s grave. I also took her to visit his family. Ricky Jr.'s parents always thanked me for bringing her to visit, and they said they were very glad to see us ahead of Shayla's graduation. Part of forgiving is understanding that you can abhor someone's actions, and still recognize their humanity. Ricky Jr. was only 20 when he shot me and killed himself. I heard from friends that Ricky Jr. had struggled with mental health issues and had been on medication, before we dated. We never lived together, so I'm not sure what Ricky Jr. endured. I never knew what meds he was taking or exactly why he needed them, I just knew I couldn't help him. Imagine if he had found more support and better outlets for his anger? Domestic violence is an epidemic problem in this country. We are failing our young women, but we are also failing our young men. We need to do better.

As I began to feel more at home in San Diego, I continued to pray for forgiveness, for myself and for others. Little by little, it was like a tight knot deep inside of me began to loosen up. I could still remember the pain, but I refused to let it overshadow my life. The more I let go of the past, the more I was able to enjoy the present and look forward to the future.

9

FAMILY

With my mom and kids at San Diego Wild Animal Park, Summer 2011

I am eternally grateful to all of my relatives and loved ones who have supported me over the years. I love my grandparents dearly. Even though our family has flaws, we have never had a shortage of affection. When my daughter Shayla graduated from college in 2019, many of our relatives flew out to be with us. When they called out Shayla's name, I swear, you could hear our family cheering for her all across the campus.

Growing up away from your parents is hard. It took me a long time to build my relationship with them. My dad lived close by, and he always stayed in touch. I never felt like I got to see him nearly enough, but I appreciated knowing he was there. My mom lived further away, so it was harder to keep up our connection. It was only after my shooting that I truly realized how much my parents loved me.

My mom was at work the day she got the call telling her that Ricky Jr. had shot me. That call changed her life forever. As I mentioned earlier, she rode in an 18-wheeler so she could be by my side. I would never call my shooting a blessing, but it did bring my mom and me closer. In recent years, we've been able to talk more about big issues. I had no idea that she had been held at gunpoint, or threatened for testifying. I'm very grateful that we have both had the chance to reconnect and heal.

Sadly, after my shooting, my dad and I did not have very much time left together. He suffered from diabetes. My dad used to pass out at the wheel sometimes when he was driving. As a toddler, I often saw him weak and struggling when he was working in the junkyard. He passed away from diabetes when he was only 44-years old. I had flown out to be by his side for over a week in September of 2001. It was my first semester of college, but I didn't care if I failed my classes. I left my kids with my aunt and uncle, and missed work and school to be with him – just like he had been there for me, when I was in the hospital. That Christmas, I drove my kids to Louisiana to see him. He was back in the hospital then, but he checked himself out during our visit. Six weeks later, he was gone.

My Dad at Shayla's first birthday party, 1997.

Our last conversation was on Valentine's Day, 2002. He told me he had received my card. We said we loved each other. He went to sleep and never woke up again. I received a call the next morning telling me that he had died. My babies and I flew out for his services, and said one last goodbye.

I learned a lot of valuable lessons from my family. They taught me to always work hard and love big. They taught me to be responsible with money and to fight for my fair share, but to always be respectful towards others. They taught me to stand up for myself, but they also taught me to me not to judge. Every single person on this planet is dealing with struggles that we don't get to see. If someone is small or mean to you, that is just a reflection of the sadness and fear inside of them. Our job is to worry about our own selves and to keep trying to add as much positivity and joy to the world as possible.

While many of these lessons nurtured me over the years, I would also come to see that some of the lessons I learned were damaging. For the women in my family, not judging people and loving big meant accepting a lot of bad behavior. If your man raises his voice, or a hand to you, you give back as good as you get, but you don't leave him. Southern values are built on tradition – for better and worse. And good Southern women stand by their men.

Maybe because of this, and because I longed for that sense of fulfillment I felt around children, I had my son Donte with a friend at school when I was only 16. By 18, I had Donte and my daughter Shayla with Ricky Jr.

I realized that I was repeating the same cycle as my parents – and many others in my family and our small town. By 18-years old, I already had two children with two different fathers – and I knew it wasn't right for me to be with either of them. Friends and relatives clucked at me, "You need a man to support you." "You've got to respect your man." In my heart, I knew, it's not right to respect someone who hurts you. It's not right to stay with a man who hits you. It's not right to be with someone if you both bring out the worst in each other.

Luckily, I was stubborn enough to go my own way. They may not have agreed with me, but my family stuck by me in so many ways. They gave me places to stay. They helped me look after my little ones so I could finish school and go to work to support us. They gave me hand-me-downs for the kids. And they've always been there for me.

In time, I was able to return some of that love. Once the kids and I were able to get a home of our own, we invited some of our younger family members and friends to live with us in San Diego for a little while, to help get them started. I wanted our home to feel warm and welcoming, like the place you want to be. We kept it stocked with lots of food for hungry teenagers, and an extra seat at the table. I wanted everyone who came there to feel like family. Our home was always open.

Family is so important. And family is more than just our relatives. We all have our dear friends and chosen family, as well. There are so many friends from my childhood and teenage years who helped support me along the way. Even though I'm far from them now, they will always be an integral part of me.

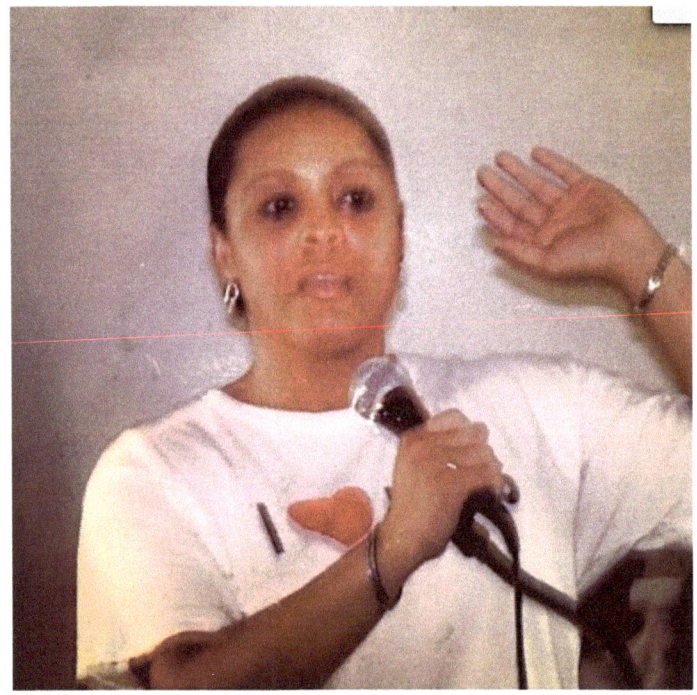

Vacation Bible School Director, 2008, San Diego, CA.
Nothing but love.

When Ms. B took me under her wing, I found a second family there with her in our church. Later, when I started my advocacy work with Everytown and Moms Demand Action, I met family all across the U.S. We have grown so divided in this country. I wish we could open our hearts a little more and see each other as real people, not just a user name on a screen.

10

FUTURE

Proud mom of a Varsity Point Guard
(my old position) and a Varsity Cheer Leader.
Donte's Senior photo, 2013.

There's no time to live in the past. My focus has always been on the future. Watching my own children grow and blossom and working with the kids at my church in San Diego has been the great joy of life.

Donte is a natural leader. He's quiet and respectful, but he has a gentle strength that can't be ignored. If someone needs something, he'll be the first to step up and give you his last. He excelled in both academics and sports, graduating on the honor roll before attending the University of Arizona, studying computer science. I coached him in basketball from the time he was four-years old and I'm so proud that his team won the State Championship. He was also a walk-on with the University of Arizona's football team the summer after he graduated from high school.

Shayla is a fighter like my mom and an old soul. I'm pretty sure this is not her first time on this earth. She was always physical, just like me, but she also has a fire and drive all her own. She took every kind of dance you can imagine and by the age of five she was already singing solo performances at our local theater and church. As a freshman in high school, Shayla was diagnosed with the same heart disease I suffered from as a child. She had to have surgery that year, but she still managed to get top grades and keep up with all of her extra-curriculars.

In high school, Shayla followed in Donte's footsteps and joined the Debate Team, eventually serving as a Teen Juror. Shayla has always had a strong innate sense of justice. She believes fiercely that everyone should be treated fairly. Shayla also spent four years as a Varsity cheerleader. I coached her cheer team, the same way I coached her brother in basketball. Shayla graduated high school with honors, just like her brother, and when it was time to go to college, she chose to study criminal justice at Cal State University Los Angeles.

We had our struggles, but I am so proud of the kind, productive people my children have become. I'm proud that they both graduated from high school with honors and I was blessed to watch my kids excel in college. I'm proud that I was able to work hard and provide a good life for my kids. I'm proud that I'm only five units short of earning my MBA.

When you come from a big family, you grow up in hand-me-downs. Not having a lot made me work harder to provide more for my kids. Even though we didn't have a lot, I knew how fortunate we all were to be alive and how much we had compared to other people. I wanted to instill a sense of gratitude and giving in my kids.

I tried to teach my kids that we do for others before we do for ourselves. A blood transfusion saved my life, so I try to give back by donating blood whenever I can. I also give presentations through the San Diego Blood Bank to Middle School, High School and young adults on the importance of blood donations. Every year on Thanksgiving, I would bring my kids to the downtown shelter to help feed the homeless before we went home for our meal. My kids excelled in school in so many areas, but I was proudest of the fact that they always received awards for kindness and best manners.

I was very grateful that my work at the church made it possible for me to always be present for Donte and Shayla. They never took a bus. I took them to every one of their practices and events, myself. I know that's not an option for all parents, but it was very important to me because of what we'd been through – and my own upbringing. I knew what it felt like to not have a parent there for parent day. You never quite feel like you're good enough. I wanted to make sure my kids knew how much I loved them and how much they had to offer the world.

No parent raises his or her children alone, though. Donte's father was not a big part of his life, and Shayla's dad was taken from her by suicide. But just like Ms. B mentored me, I always made sure that my children had strong role models to help give them the discipline and guidance to succeed. I am so grateful to my aunt and uncle, and to all of my children's coaches and teachers for all that they did to help my children grow into such fine adults.

Shayla and Donte, the loves of my life.
Summer, 2019.

Part of the reason I love being around young people so much is because they always inspire me to stay positive and keep going. I'm so proud of the adults my children have grown into, but like a lot of parents, once they moved out, I found myself searching a little for my purpose. I was working towards my MBA, but I still felt drawn to seek out something more. Now that my kids didn't need me all the time, I wondered how could I be of service?

I tried not to talk to my kids too much about what happened to me, but they knew Shayla's father had shot me before he killed himself. I never wanted anything I said to hurt anyone or stop Shayla from feeling love for her father. But I know it's made an impact on my kids' lives. In her criminal justice studies, I think it probably hit Shayla even harder that I was shot five times and lived to tell my tale.

I grew up with guns. My grandpa worked for the Sheriff's Department. I know how important they are to many people in our country, but Everytown and Moms Demand Action are not anti-gun. In fact, many of their members are responsible gun owners, themselves. They are not trying to repeal the Second Amendment. They respect people's right to protect their families. They advocate for common sense gun laws - mostly on the local level - to help make all of us a little safer. They also work to ensure that people are as informed as possible about gun safety issues. They recognize that the laws we need in a big city like Chicago might not be the same laws that are needed in rural Tennessee.

Reading about Everytown and Moms Demand Action, I felt a little bit of that light I'd felt in the hospital shining inside of me. I'm naturally a little shy. I'm upbeat, but I don't tend to put myself out there in public all that much. But I remembered how much joy I felt when I had the breakthrough working with little ones at the church, and I felt that nudge in my gut telling me that if I could be brave enough to share my story, it *might* make a difference to other people going through hard times. Ms. B taught me your voice is so powerful, and if you ever have the chance to share it, you should give it your all.

I got in touch with Moms Demand Action and discovered that they have a group specifically for survivors of gun violence. I've met so many incredible, strong survivors through that group. Many of them have lost loved ones to gun violence and some of them have survived it, just like me. There are so many powerful voices out there. No matter what your history or political affiliation, if you get the chance, please take a few moments to listen to some of these survivors. Every time I hear one of them speak, I am deeply moved. I nearly lost my life, but I can't imagine the pain of losing a child or a loved one to senseless gun violence. I truly believe, we can honor the Second Amendment and still find ways to make our cities, schools and streets a little safer.

It was hard for me to get up in front of a crowd for the first time to share my story, but I joined Moms Demand Action for my kids. The day Ricky Jr. shot me; Donte and Shayla nearly lost their mother. My daughter did lose her father that day to suicide – something that happens far too often in this country. I wanted to tell my story, but I wanted to focus on the love and hope and redemption that we can build together, not just on loss and gun violence.

In October of 2017, I was invited to speak at the Brady Campaign Summit. I had shared my story many times by then, but I had never delivered it in front of my children. Watching my daughter cry while I talked about everything I'd been though, how hard I'd had to fight to get back to her and her brother, I felt like I truly felt the weight of my own story for the first time.

It's still hard for me to put myself out there. I have received such a warm welcome every time I've told my story and I've connected with so many people who told me how much it meant to them, but part of me still held back. There are so many powerful survivors I've met who have lost their loved ones to gun violence. Shayla and Donte and I are still here. Who was I to think that my story mattered? Every time I find myself in that place, I remind myself that I do this for the children. The adults in this country have let far too many of their own get shot in our streets and schools. Young people in America deserve better than to live in fear because their parents and grandparents are too afraid to have an adult conversation.

I initially got involved in this movement for my own children, but I've been so moved watching the way the younger generation is getting involved. The Parkland kids and the student activists from Chicago, and many other cities, are speaking up and saying things that we adults have been afraid to say for far too long. They are the future and they inspire me to do more.

So, I decided to write my story down and share it. My hope is that we can open up a real adult dialogue on gun sense laws in this country. We were shocked by Columbine and Sandy Hook, but still we were too afraid to act. We've allowed school shootings to become so common, that many of our kids now say they expect one to happen at their school. And the bleak reality is, school shootings and mass shootings are only a fraction of the shootings in this country. Americans are getting shot on our streets and in our homes every single day. Together, we have the power to do something about that.

Many gun violence survivors have to live with bullets inside their bodies – bullets that are slowly poisoning us with lead. I have to test the level of lead in my blood on a regular basis. I recently had yet another in a long line of surgeries. I've been on steroids. That is the reality that gun violence survivors live with every day. We all pay the price for that. Gun violence is estimated to cost America $229 billion dollars every year.

If you survive the initial shooting, there are still years of pain and suffering ahead. Scars, both visible and invisible. Beyond the health care costs, there are additional tolls. Over the years, I have lost jobs when I was really struggling with pain, including a good job at JP Morgan Chase bank. Many survivors of mass shootings struggle every day with survivors' guilt. Some take their own lives. We can do something about that if more of us rise up and take a stand together.

I would like to thank Shannon Watts for starting Moms Demand Action for Gun Sense in America. Thank you for giving everyday Americans a platform to raise our voices together for common sense gun laws. According to a recent Quinnipiac poll, 73% of Americans believe that we should be doing more to address gun violence.

Obviously, gun sense is very important to me, but I hope that anyone going through a hard time will find strength in the five powers I leaned on to help me survive.

After the hospital told me that they would never be able to remove the bullets inside my body, I decided to name them – FAITH, FIGHT, FORGET, FORGIVE and FAMILY. Naming them meant the bullets no longer had power over me. Instead, they remind me of the resilience and love I discovered within to help me survive. I believe that each of us has these powers inside of us – to help us heal, to help us grow, and to help us flourish. When I tell my story now, I always say I'm carrying all five bullets for life, but I'm so blessed to be able to walk and talk 23 years later. I intend to make the most of this life.

Thank you so much for listening to my story. If you're struggling, I hope you can find the strength within yourself to rise stronger. Here are some resources I've collected over the years, as a well as a journal to help you tell your own story.

Collage of me speaking at the Parkland School Walkout in San Diego, CA, Donte's football game, 2018, with Shayla, 2018, and speaking at a Moms Demand Action meeting in the San Fernando Valley, 2018.

THE POWER OF FIVE RESOURCES

First and foremost, here are some important numbers for anyone struggling:

National Suicide Prevention Hotline: 1-800-273-8255

Grief Recovery Helpline: 1-800-445-4808

National Domestic Violence Hotline: 1-800-799-7233

Trevor Project (Suicide hotline for LGBTQ youth): 1-866-488-7386

Text to join Moms Demand Action: 644-33

National Center for Post-Traumatic Stress Disorder Info Line: 1-802-296-6300

Staples Center, 2020, with Shayla.

Please, also reach out locally to school counselors, social workers, clergy, women's shelters, or any other services you might need. Always remember, you are not alone.

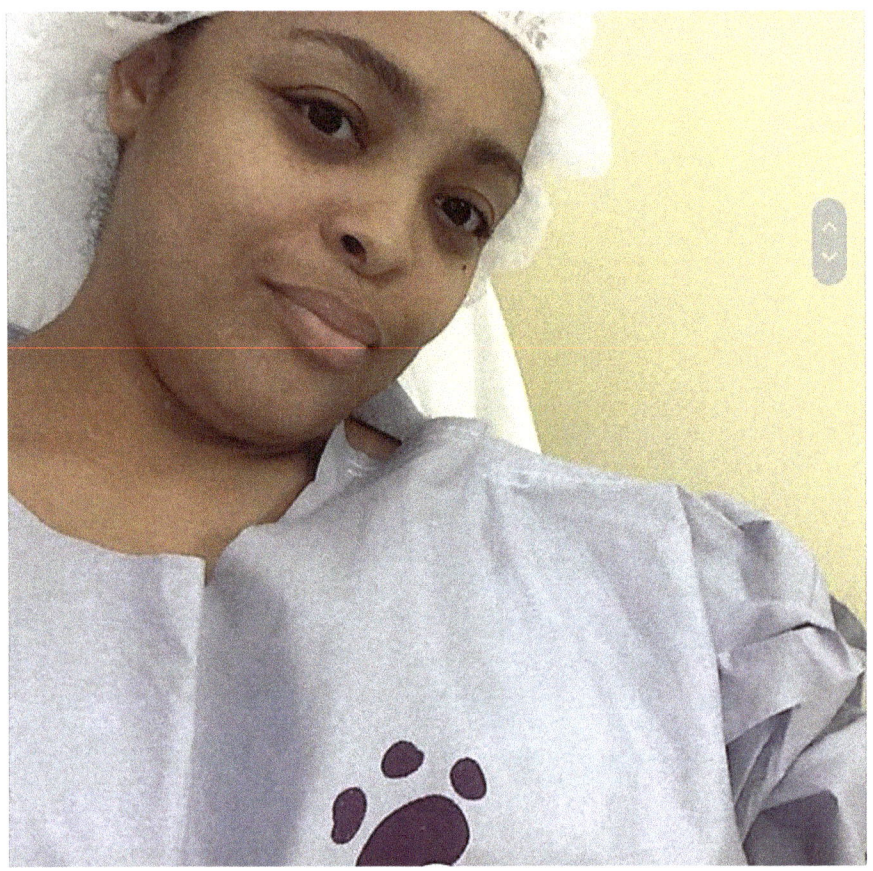

Surgery in 2015, San Diego, CA. Gun violence survivors often have to endure many years of surgery, as well as the threat of lead poisoning.

FAITH – If you are struggling with something, and you are so inclined, faith can be a really powerful way to connect. You don't have to have a religious epiphany like I did. People find spiritual comfort in many ways, churches, synagogues, mosques, temples, nature, meditation, or simply trying to live a good life. Wherever you find that spark, it is a powerful feeling to open yourself up to feeling connected to something bigger than yourself. The more people I meet telling my story, the more I realize how much we are all connected. The whole world is truly one big family.

1. <u>Religious suggestions</u> - If you are religious like me, find a church that you like. Try out a few different ones and see which one feels like home to you. If you feel like you're craving something spiritual, but you're not quite sure what you're looking for, try visiting a few different faiths.

2. <u>Spiritual suggestions -</u> If you feel spiritual, but you don't feel connected to organized religion, there are lots of ways to tap into that feeling outside of a church setting. Go for a hike, take some yoga classes, visit a sound bath – whatever speaks to your soul.

3. <u>Atheist suggestions -</u> If you're an atheist, but you still want to just marvel in the wonder of the world, some of the above things might work for you, as well. If you miss a sense of community, maybe consider joining a 'meet up' group in your area. If you like being outdoors, consider taking up gardening, or go to a star gazing event. One of the things I love about being in church is that it makes me forget about my own worries for a little while, and feel a connection to something much bigger than myself. There are plenty of ways to connect with vastness outside of a church setting.

Mom's Demand Action 5th anniversary bake sales, 2018. Orange County, CA.

FIGHT – there's a fighter inside each of us. Sometimes, we all need to tap into our inner strength. The question is, how do we use that power for good? How do we fight lovingly and peacefully for the things that matter to us? I know that my athletic background and my positive outlook on life helped me to heal. Sooner or later, we will all face challenges, but do whatever you can to take care of yourself, both mentally and physically.

Presenting as a Trainer at GSU in Washington, D.C., 2019.

What could FIGHT look like in your daily life?

1. <u>Stay active</u>. As a child, I was a natural athlete. Like all gifts, it came so easily to me, that I totally took it for granted, but now I cherish the power of movement. I

can't dance or run like I used to, but I walk and exercise every chance I get. If you're going through something difficult, try to stay as active as you can. That might just mean slow strolls or light physical therapy, but do whatever you can do to keep your body strong. Your mind and mood will follow. If you're healthy and going through a tough time, like a divorce or another big life change, I highly recommend something more strenuous – take a kick boxing class, or join a team sport.

2. <u>Join a political group</u>. Gather together with people with your same values and stand up for the things you believe in.

3. <u>Seek out therapy.</u> You don't have to do everything alone. If you're going through a really stressful time, there's no shame in reaching out for help. In fact, it's the brave thing to do. There are LOTS of therapy situations out there – group therapy, and clinics that see patients on a sliding scale.

At home in San Diego, CA with my kids, 2011.

FORGET – Forgetting doesn't mean that you literally forget the bad things that happen to you. It's about finding ways to take away their power. I didn't bad mouth Ricky Jr. to my kids. I tell my story to help others avoid gun violence, or to help them get out of abusive relationships, but I try not to ever wallow in regret or self-pity. Focus on the things you love and the things that bring you joy, no matter how small they might be. I made it back to my family. I got to see my babies grow up. I know what a great gift I've been given and how valuable every moment is. Let go of the pain in your past and keep focusing on the promise of your future.

Our country has become so divided, but I believe at our core, we are a country full of people who care about each other. I taught my children that each of us has five fingers on our hands. Those five fingers represent the five powers within us. We can choose every day how we use the strength in our hands. Will we help lift each other up, or will we try to hold each other back and keep each other down? I truly hope that we join hands and work together to help our whole nation rise to its highest potential.

There are many opportunities to help lift people in your community. Not only will you do good for someone else, but studies show that volunteering is one of the best ways to boost your own mood.

Participating in Senator Feinstein's Roundtable with Survivors on Gun Safety, March 27, 2018.

1. Volunteer for a homeless shelter, a woman's shelter, an elderly home, or at a school. Even if it's just for a few hours, every couple of months. The best way to forget about your own troubles is to help someone else for a little while with theirs.
2. If you're athletically inclined, consider helping coach a sports team, or becoming a Big Brother or Sister. As a

single mom, I can tell you that every single coach in my kids' lives made a huge impact.

3. If you love animals, volunteer at a shelter – or assist with adoption days.
4. Volunteer for a clean up day at the beach or river near you, or even on the main street of your town. Take pride in your community and get to know your neighbors.
5. Donate blood. There is a vital need for blood donors. Please consider donating to the Red Cross, or any local hospital and help save a life.
6. Be open to new people, even if they push you outside of your comfort zone. You can maintain your own values and beliefs and still respect others. Just watch Queer Eye! The powers that be try to make us afraid of each other. Our news is slanted, our politicians are unreliable. But the truth is, we are all neighbors. And opening yourself up to a perfect stranger who is totally different from you might change your whole life.

Summer, 1996, a few months prior to the shooting.

FORGIVE - This is probably our most important power – and the hardest one to achieve. The people we love sometimes hurt us a lot, or disappoint us. Sometimes, we even disappoint ourselves. We are only human. In the long run, holding on to anger and resentment and shame only hurts us. It was hard for me to bring my daughter to visit the grave of the man who caused me so much pain, but I knew it was important for my daughter. I don't go there on my own now that she is grown, but I learned that you can honor the pain that you feel without letting it eat away at you.

Forgiveness is one of the hardest and most powerful things we can do for ourselves. Here are some suggestions for incorporating it into your life.

1. <u>Rituals for Letting Go.</u> Forgiveness is an ongoing process for me. Prayer and church have obviously been very helpful for me, but if you're not religious, I think there is still power in creating a ritual for yourself so that you can physically let go of your anger, as well as mentally. Maybe you could light a candle and then blow it out when you say that you are forgiving someone, or letting them go. Or, you could buy wish papers, light them on fire and watch them burn away to symbolize your forgiveness.

2. <u>Annual Forgiveness</u>. I love the idea of Lent and Ramadan and any regular system of forgiveness. There is power in setting aside a specific time of year to reflect on forgiveness, both for yourself, and others. If you're not religious, maybe you could pick a time that feels right to you.

3. <u>Forgiving isn't forgetting</u>. If somebody really hurt you, remember that forgiving isn't the same thing as forgetting. Forgiving someone is more about refusing to allow them to take up your emotional space. When you forgive someone for causing you pain and anger, you open up space inside of yourself to fill with love and joy and friendship. It also doesn't hurt to step back and try to be the bigger person. We are all human and we're all doing the best we can. People might make mistakes and still really love you. Or they may be dealing with past traumas of their own that make them incapable of treating you the way you deserve. Forgive them. But never forget to protect yourself.

Brady State Conference in San Diego, CA, September, 2017.

FAMILY - Maybe you're like me, and you come from a big loving messy family. Maybe you have a close circle of friends who help see you through. Maybe your kids are your whole world, or you get lots of love from your fur babies. Family can mean a lot of things to different people, but humans are social creatures - we need to connect with others. I hope you have the support you need, but if not, try to reach out. Volunteer a little of your time, if you can, or join a group. When I was in a coma, I wanted to give in so many times, but the thought of getting back to my babies, and hearing the voices of my loved ones, gave me the strength to keep going.

How can you stay connected with your family?

1. Eat together. Plan at least one sit down family dinner every week, with no electronics or other distractions allowed. Research has shown that there are many benefits to families eating dinner together. I get it, our modern lives are busy, but even one family meal per week can make a big difference.

2. Play together. Play sports together, get out for a hike, play a board game, go and see an event. Make sure you connect with your family while having fun.

3. Extend an invitation. Try to connect with your extended family as often as you can. Plan a family picnic, or if you live in different cities, make a Skype date. If you're on good terms with your family, extended family relationships can mean a lot to you and your children.

11

FAREWELL FOR NOW

College Graduation, 2011.
My name is La'Shea Cretain. I am a gun violence survivor. I lived to tell my story.

The past few years have been a whirlwind. Our country seems to be in a constant state of conflict and chaos. In the midst of all the turmoil, I have also experienced great personal joy. I'm close to finishing my Master's degree. I have done things through my work with Moms Demand Action that I never would have dreamed possible. I found the strength to tell my story in front of a hundred people at the Brady Conference, including my babies. Since then, I have spoken in front of thousands of people all around the country - including back home in Louisiana. I've helped train our new fellows class through Moms Demand Action, assisting others with sharing their stories. I have advocated for new laws in our state capitol. I have told my story in front of famous celebrities, and questioned presidential candidates. I've met an extended family of warriors fighting to make us all safer. I've also had the honor of meeting some of my personal heroes, including Anita Hill and Common. I've been invited to attend many NBA games, including watching my favorite team, The Golden State Warriors.

I'm still trying to find my balance, and I know a lot of you are, too. Stand up whenever you can, and give yourself a break when you need it. Trust that others will carry the load for a little while. Each of us has so much potential inside of us. Ms. B was right – your voice is important. You are important. I hope that you find the spark inside of yourself to see that, and to share all of your strength and beauty with the world. It's time for all of us to heal, and to use the power within to help lift each other up.

ABOUT THE AUTHOR

La'Shea Cretain is a mother, faith counselor, activist and a popular motivational speaker. She has spoken at events for Everytown and Moms Demand Action for Gun Sense in America, The Brady Campaign, and Women's Day. Her story has been published in both the New York Times and Vogue, Her uplifting and empowering message of turning adversity into your own inner-strength has inspired everyone who has ever heard her speak. Now, she is sharing her story with the world.

Feel free to share your own story here!

Feel free to share your own story here!

Feel free to share your own story here!

Feel free to share your own story here!

Feel free to share your own story here!

Feel free to share your own story here!

Feel free to share your own story here!

Feel free to share your own story here!

Feel free to share your own story here!

Feel free to share your own story here!

Draw your own art work here!

Draw your own art work here!

Draw your own art work here!

Draw your own art work here!

Draw your own art work here!

Draw your own art work here!

Draw your own art work here!

Draw your own art work here!

Draw your own art work here!

Draw your own art work here!

Anything else you feel inspired to do to turn your pain into purpose!

Anything else you feel inspired to do to turn your pain into purpose!

Anything else you feel inspired to do to turn your pain into purpose!

Anything else you feel inspired to do to turn your pain into purpose!

Anything else you feel inspired to do to turn your pain into purpose!

What does this word mean to you?
FAITH

What does this word mean to you?

FIGHT

What does this word mean to you?
FORGET

What does this word mean to you?
FORGIVE

What does this word mean to you?
FAMILY

IT'S UP TO YOU!

"My story may be your story, there's always a way out, never give up on the fight, always stay connected to family, believe in yourself, forgiveness is not for the other person it's for you, and never forget."

- La'Shea Cretain

In dark times we don't always see the light. Where does your HOPE come from?

H _____

O _____

P _____

E _____

I LOVE YOU!!!

REFERENCE

Keeping Up with the Kardashians, Season 12, Episode 20 (pg. 9)

Jenny Holzer, *Vigil* Light Project (pg.10)

Brady Campaign, bradyunited.com, key statistics (pg.17)

Mark Follman, Julia Lurie, Jaeah Lee, and James West (April 15, 2015) The True Cost of Gun Violence in America. *Mother Jones* (pg. 18)

www.ingramcontent.com/pod-product-compliance
Lightning Source LLC
Chambersburg PA
CBHW042117100526
44587CB00025B/4091